Bass Fis

for Beginners

A Beginner's Guide to the Basics and the Necessary Skills for Bass Fishing to Become an Angler Who Uses the Right Techiques and Tricks in Every Season to Hook the Big One

By Eli Leander

© **Copyright 2019 - All rights reserved.**

The content contained within this book may not be reproduced, duplicated or transmitted without direct written permission from the author or the publisher.

Under no circumstances will any blame or legal responsibility be held against the publisher or author for any damages, reparation, or monetary loss due to the information contained within this book. Either directly or indirectly.

Legal Notice:

This book is copyright protected. This book is only for personal use. You cannot amend, distribute, sell, use, quote or paraphrase any part, or the content within this book, without the consent of the author or publisher.

Disclaimer Notice:

Please note the information contained within this document is for educational and entertainment purposes only. All effort has been executed to present accurate, up to date and reliable, complete information. No warranties of any kind are declared or implied. Readers acknowledge that the author is not engaging in the rendering of legal, financial, medical or professional advice. The content within this book has been derived from various sources. Please consult a licensed professional before attempting any techniques outlined in this book.

By reading this document, the reader agrees that under no

circumstances is the author responsible for any losses, direct or indirect, which are incurred as a result of the use of information contained within this document, including, but not limited to, —errors, omissions, or inaccuracies.

Contents

Foreword 1
  Bass Explained 1
Introduction 9
  Where to Find the Bass 9
Chapter 1 - Bass Fishing 101 14
  Tools 21
  Environmental Factors 44
    Temperature 47
    Water Condition 48
    Noise/Vibrations/Disturbances 49
    Color, Time of day, Sunlight 50
    Time of Year 51
    Predatory Nature 53
    Favorite habitat 54
    Natural Diet 55
    Confidence 55
  Bass Fishing Tricks 56
    Precise Casting 56
    Landing Fish 60
    Lure-Fishing and Spinning 62
    Plastic Worms 65
Chapter 2 - Mistakes and Tricks 66
Chapter 3 - Bass Fishing Styles 69
  Skipping 69

Ripping 70
　　Drift Trolling 70
　　Fly-Rodding 71
　　Night and Ice-fishing 71
Conclusion 73
　　Catch-and-Release 73
Glossary 75

Thank you for buying this book and I hope that you will find it useful. If you will want to share your thoughts on this book, you can do so by leaving a review on the Amazon page, it helps me out a lot.

Foreword

Bass Explained

Whichever the reason you had for getting this book, you are certain to discover a quenching reprieve. Quench your thirst for knowledge about any bass fishing challenge, endeavor or battle, you are going to or may deal within your life. There are thing for everybody within this guide!

If your primary interest, is enhancing your capability to capture Bass, improving, (and perhaps) even stacking the chances in your favor of being successful time and again, each time, in this angling venture and any upcoming expedition you intend to carry out, then this guide has something valuable to provide you.

When you are after the Bass, understanding the fundamentals resembles the lifeline of your approach, bringing your odds alive with each cast!

ADDITIONALLY, find and establish YOUR OWN sportsman-like, angling character and style, while slowly developing your gratitude and understanding of the outdoors, as part of your fishing journey.

I provide a practical approach to the complexities and intricacies associated with this prominent sport. I hope that this is captured properly by the brief title.

The focus, approach, goals and objectives are straightforward-- the premise and basis even simpler: to find out the fundamentals, get them right, regularly, with mastery and skill, and they are going to ultimately lead you to catch all the Bass you can actually desire!

I prefer to get right to the subject and aspects of our conversation-- how to discover and catch Bass! Basic yet in-depth, the text is composed in such a way, that it could be applied immediately, without devoting hours toreading and going through pages of information.

The majority of accomplished authors and published works, illustrate Bass fishing as the supreme angling experience and 'The Bass' (predator- hunter itself), as rough, unforeseeable, with a powerful survival instinct, sensing/sensors, fantastic awareness, and that is what makes them the efficient and keen hunters.

These fish gain from natures' presents of powerful hearing, sight, maneuverability, substantial speed, and even jumping action moves that are going to have you catch your breath ... with wonder and exhilaration that is! All of this renders it feasible for the Bass to measure up to its name and track record, as one of the gaming fish extremes and each angler's dream prize!

Part of the Percichthyidae family (additionally sub-divided into the genus Morone-- looked at a different branch or unit (white, striped, yellow), they are commonly distributed in tropical and temperate waters, sub-species to be discovered in saltwater and fresh water. There are additionally the European sea bass (Dicentrarchus labrax) and Australian bass (Acquaria novemaculeate),.

Their natural diet and food of choice consists of little fish, shellfishes, worms and bugs-- certain anglers have actually additionally had terrific success with live-bait, such as frogs and eels.

Then you have the black bass, jointly described and including our treasured target-- said by some to be the most sporting species in The United States and Canada—the Centrarchidae family. (Smallmouth and largemouth bass, spotted, redeye, black bass, striped, Quadalupee, Suwannee).

Synthetic baits have proven helpful to the majority of anglers. Live baits are ideal, yet these fish can be lured, teased and drawn to strike with synthetic ones like spoons, spinners, surface plugs, crank-baits, and plastic worms-- more on this a little later. Understanding what to pick (and WHY), use, switch to in particular conditions, and how to maximize this sort of allure, is a crucial fundamental aspect for each striving or fantastic angler alike.

These fishes are all predatory, warming to artificial lures and natural baits. A lot of anglers would recommend trolling or spinning for freshwater fishing for Bass (bigger species) and fly-fishing or spinning for the tinier species. Saltwater aficionados may likewise take into consideration trolling, tide fishing or surfcasting.

Fishing for and catching Bass, in numerous waters around the world, has a proud history and custom. The majority of us are too happy to get involved in and form aspect of it, whether from boat, coast, rocks or streams, rivers, oceans or lakes. We like to tell our magnificent tales and ponder how to alter and modify, adjust and/or develop brand-new strategies, approaches to hook large-mouth, smallmouth, spotted, speckled, striped and black bass. You choose your favorite. To each of his own.

Understanding how to tell a large-mouth bass from a smallmouth, spotted from striped and so forth, is an extremely fundamental ability most anglers master rapidly. Looking particularly at the physical features and size are excellent locations to begin. Train your eye to 'find the distinctions,' so to speak.

They vary in size, dorsal fins, and markings, for instance. Their upper jaws don't have the same length and their dorsal fins are not identical. The large-mouth comes with a spiny dorsal fin, largest in the center part, with practically a unique 'break,' right prior to the second dorsal fins set begin. For our buddies, the smallmouth bass, these fins are more flat, second and first are linked, with special scales at the bottom of the second dorsal fins set.

Apart from understanding the differences between fish species, by physical qualities and/or sights, there is some basic guidance I can offer right here. Treading gently, experiencing and honoring nature, the great outdoors, complying with the anglers' catch and release code, environmental protection for angler generations to come, and so on are all greatly essential in your angling undertakings.

Second, preserving a general awareness, what some call "reading the waters" (comprehending the body of water, fish habitat, shape, temperature level, depth, stratified levels and so on), being usually, along with particularly 'observant', equipping yourself with understanding, capability and knowledge of the environment and the species, and all other pertinent elements to your fishing activity and endeavors-- critical for effective process and result.

Lastly, (and nearly most notably), stay versatile, for change is a huge part of this satisfying outdoor activity. It is absolutely not for the reckless or the faint of heart!

Introduction

Where to Find the Bass

How to capture Bass and then capture additional, bigger bass, more frequently, in more locations, more consistently, having a proactive strategy, stacking the odds in your favor to prosper, catching additional fish and taking pleasure in the process, is what this fundamental book deals with.

The hunter ends up being the hunted-- find out how a small paradigm shift, could cause success with bass! Begin thinking as the watery hunter, be and comprehend the bass from the hunter's perspective. Observe, know, study, follow, and utilize its natural routine, patterns, preferences, practices, prey and food selection, and you are going to have have some fascinating stories to share.

If you were informed that there is one specific fish species that the majority would refer to as rough, wise, outwitting and elusively difficult to capture, then it's the Bass-- in all its sizes, shapes, versions and sub-categories.

It rings true, regardless of the body of water, context, special and/or any scenario or condition, despite tricks, pointers, proven science, strategy and all the intent in the world! Bass fishing is tough and gratifying simultaneously. To guarantee hours of countless satisfaction, follow the guidelines (and add a few of your own here as well!) offered here and be prepared to hook the next huge one ... consistently.

There are numerous aspects, operating in mix with the science and art, pursuit and sport that is Bass Fishing! Synergy and strategy , add to ultimate, and (I would argue), repeatable and consistent success. Tools, site, lure and ability, dusk or dawn, deep or shallow waters, saltwater/salt, from boat or coast-- it matters not! There are tricks and methods for each of them.

Beginners, novices, seasonal and experienced anglers alike, are all invited to read this book to find some wonderful, in-demand facts regarding bass fishing! Eventually, it is as much about the process, pleasure, admiration and understanding, as it is about the fish!

End up being a watchful, student of nature, the Bass' patterns and routines, whether utilizing trolling, synthetic and/or live bait, on ice, salt and fresh, shallow and deep waters, do so, utilizing all to your benefit, as you go on your own Bass journey!

Bass is, without a doubt, the most commonly circulated fish in North America-- often because of the convenience of our mobility and hectic society, tailored for transportation and travel, Bass is within grasp. Small-mouths, Large-mouths, spotted, stripped, black bass, and so on all await.

Ever heard of a clever fish which makes measured, in-the-moment choices? One whose survival impulse is so powerful that it snatches and, at other times, absolutely disregards things and hangs around apparently withdrawn, just to bite/strike when least anticipated!

Well, that would be common of our flaky, finned fish, the 'Bass.' For the purposes of this guide, this species takes center-stage-- this is intentional and deliberate. Bass fishing has to do with precisely that. Erratic, tenacious, and a challenge to the majority of us.

Numerous researchers have actually verified that Bass nearly 'compute' the quantity of energy it is going to take them to pursue the prey vs. the return. If this holds true and confirmed, what are the ramifications for anglers? We need to outmaneuver them, obviously! It is all in the fundamentals, the techniques, battle strategy, tease, allure, and strategies we select to utilize in this process. This is going to determine and dictate our success.

Chapter 1 - Bass Fishing 101

Many, if not all of the so-called 'insider' tricks, pointers and stories to tell of huge Bass hauls, all revolve, around an extremely straightforward fundamental guideline-- comprehending the fish, (their life-cycles, feeding choices, routines and patterns and food selection, their relationship with the overall eco-system, their nature, and place on the food-chain, timing it important.

In actuality, you are setting about, producing the most favorable angling procedure and the result you can manage!

Bass fishing is a fascination, an art and science. It interests old and young, draws in anglers from all over and all sides of the amateur and professional continuum.

One secret to bass fishing is what we can quickly call, 'predictable habits.' Patterns, habits, life cycles, the natural tempo that is nature and life -- additionally relates to fish. This suggests that Bass exist within this natural actuality. If you could profit from comprehending it more, you are going to boost your odds of effective hooks/bites.

Looking for cover, foraging among stumps, rocks, weeds, sometimes on the prowl searching for prey, other times simply 'lunching' around delicately, all appear to be part of The Bass feeding repertoire and routines. Taking advantage and taking this into consideration when beginning and whenever casting is going to benefit you significantly.

Another is "competitive advantage," The Bass have an "airtight sac" (breathing bladder), which can inflate, that allows it to swim and prosper at various levels.

A strong tail aids with agility, maneuverability and speed. It could reach considerable depths.

Other aspects such as time of day, water clarity, controlled sunshine, vibration sensing, water displacement, sound level of sensitivity, all contribute to this fish's shrewd and making sure that you scrutinize these hints is going to boost your chances of hooking your following huge one.

Uncovering, for instance, how The Bass senses and chooses shade and color at the moment, can regularly additionally aid anglers to boost their performance. The choice and kind of colors, lure and motion, bait, and so on can all add considerably to your efforts.

Where the fish are ... everybody is going to have an answer or at least their experience/opinion on what/where/when. Nonetheless, in some cases, it is as straightforward as comprehending the habitat and those that live and prosper in it, to better engage with and delight in fishing in it-

- a kind of exploring the depths, in a manner of speaking. For instance: the water temperature and available oxygen determine disbursement and moving patterns of fish species. Feeding preferences and routines are different, falling more on the live or alive-looking bait. Some quote smallmouth bass, as revealing an inclination for crawfish and utilizing that as an 'indication' of where these critters are going to be discovered, on the hunt for their preferred snack! Taking a look at stomach content of fish you have actually captured and kept, holds concealed hints about the food of choice, crawfish, whitefish and others.

Having confidence, ability AND the appropriate mindset when Bass fishing is essential. In this fight to outsmart your opponent, you are going to require each tool and technique available to make an effective catch. Never get dissuaded, feel defeated, or worse, give up. Bad days occur to each angler. Nature does things its way, you need to find and delight in the rhythm you are so delicately part of.

Practice is key-- there is no shortcut, quick-fish technique for $19.99, that can ensure you bites and more bass constantly, anytime. It DOES take effort and dedication, determination and rigor from the angler. Certain days are going to be better than others. Regardless of the process, conditions and result, on a certain day put all of it down to lessons learned and experience. Learn and log , grow and share, in your own knowledge, toolkit and confidence, as a devoted bass angler.

Another crucial technique is, in fact, NO TECHNIQUE WHATSOEVER-- we call it a learned skill. It takes more of that effort we discussed before! Specific, fixed casting demands target-precision practice, enhancing your capability to put the lure precisely where you would wish it to be-- let us refer to it as 'hitting the mark.' This is another essential technique and method you can practice in your living room or in the park; attempt utilizing plugs and improve each time at regularly striking your target.

Coming to be and being a proactive attendee in the environment and context, understanding when to carry on, alter something and/or stop for the time-being (holding off the hunt or resting when needed, preparing your approach for the following trip out), is what it all comes to.

Habitual animals of comfort, The Bass (as a species), are not a lot different than a contemporary guy. Having this in mind is going to assist you as well, as an angler. We enjoy what we enjoy, how and when we enjoy it and typically desire it on time, when it is there and prepared, be safe, delight in life and we yearn for comfort-- shelter, food and wellness! Does this seem a great deal different from our own requirements and needs? Not truly! Well, that is one method of evening the odds.

Comprehending the fundamental needs and niceties for these watery "animals," holds hints and advantages, for every and any angler.

Stimulus, pattern, regimen, routine-- predictors and hints-- your trump card when absolutely nothing else functions! Learn and establish abilities, to 'read' (rapidly at a glimpse, observe and make a judgment), understand intuitively what is going to occur, next and why-- find the pattern out, stay with it and exploit it to your benefit and angling success. Meet the Bass where they are, accommodate their requirements and you are going to be shocked at what you encounter in the waters beneath!

Familiarity with the Bass' favored locations to spend time is crucial to succeed: Stumps, bottoms, logs, trees, plants and weeds, shapes, structures, travel- paths, creeks, deeper passages/shallows, channels, coves, bluffs, banks and coastlines-- all could be repeating hints on regular, predictable habits of the bass. The majority of the 'pros' got their understanding through reading, studying habits of their catch, in a really comparable fashion than what you are carrying out. Each time you get to know your fishy buddies a bit better, up until you understand intuitively where they are going to be and where their favorite locations are. Understanding and heading where the fish are ends up being demystified, and much more amazing, for it is now more than an inkling or sudden chance-- it is an organized encounter where the watery hunter ends up being the hunted!

Tools

Having the appropriate tools, understanding how to utilize them ideally, how and when, (additionally how not to utilize them and what they are not appropriate for) can all aid you with your bass fishing journey.

The fundamentals relating to rods, line, reels, weights, hooks, sinkers, bobbers, sensors, lures and other tools (vests, hats, nets, aromas, scissors, and so on), offer you an appreciation for having the appropriate tools for the job(s) ahead.

As an extremely participatory and stimulating sport, Bass fishing is simply nearly unrivaled in the large number of tools and styles to utilize. From peaceful streams, serene lakes to rushing rivers and open sea, there is a thing for everybody.

If you are searching for fast pointers on the best tools, most fit to your goals and the methods to master to capture bass in any situation, may this next part inform and motivate you, as you dive right into the 'utilities of the fishing trade.' Several bass fishing tools, we are going to be concentrating on are:

- Reels, Rods, Hooks and Lines.

- Tackle: Bait and Lures, Artificial and Live.

Restricted space does not allow big comparative descriptions or rants on the benefit of certain tools above others. These debates are well published and popular in the present literature.

We take a more functional strategy and take a look at what you are going to, in fact, require to hook your next huge one, without hoping for luck! I'd like to mention that selecting the appropriate tools means a great deal of various things to various individuals. Each angler has actually his/her own interpretation of what that means, varying ability level, physical qualities and Weaknesses/strengths, so I am not going to proclaim understanding what is appropriate for you. What I do provide are simple recommendations on which tools are going to aid you indulge in rigging, preparing, hooking/baiting, recovering and landing the next big one!

Even when you explore your environments and the marvel of species of fish and their life cycles, habits and patterns experimenting with your tools and what is offered to anglers these days, is part of the amazing Bass fishing world. From sensors, fish-finders, temperature level gauges, and superior technologies, to the art of preparing your hooks and lines, selecting the bait/lures most matched to your situation and function and more, contributes to the enjoyment and excitement of the activity. Prepping yourself with an understanding of these, are going to increase your self-confidence and practicing frequently is going to pay off over time as your know-how, exposure and fishing proficiency grows.

When it pertains to tools, the viewpoints are many and far between. Your condition, situation, purpose and objective are all going to figure into the last choice (oh, yes, and do not overlook the constantly-present spending plan and price)!

Baitcasting or spinning with synthetic lures, and teasing with live-baits, are all choices offered to you, with professional tools on hand to help you. Usually, a 6 to 7 feet rod (baitcasting or spinning), with a fitting reel with 6 to 10-pound line, fast taper, single-action reel would help you a great deal. Weed-less hooks are a lifesaver in really thick weeds or cover.

Angling methods and tackle keep refining, establishing and those things nearly take on a life of its own for each single angler. There is not truly a method for everyone. This individualized relationship with your tools may imply a fundamental rod to begin with, and after that, including a couple for your various expeditions and excursions-- your Bass journey has just begun. There are modern tackles and techniques, conventional or innovative, enabled and technology-driven, whatever you like or favor, there is a thing for each budget and taste.

It is an old sport, many engage in it, with echoes of early anglers and hunters living off the land. Experiencing that timeline via involved activity, such as bass fishing is really fulfilling. Many novices could be overwhelmed by the choice of tools available on the marketplace currently. Understanding what to choose/purchase, when and how to (ideally) apply, utilize it properly, to make the most of your odds of capturing your next huge one is crucial.

High quality tackle is necessary-- it needs to be sufficient for whatever nature tosses your way. You are going to want to develop your toolbox of knowledge and tools in time, to react best to a few of the obstacles at hand. Excellent suitable lures and baits and how to utilize them successfully, in mix, in fast succession to guarantee bites, are other crucial elements, as is significance of preparing, presenting well, precise hooking, casting (sharpening the hooks and turning them up somewhat to make sure that the fish remain on hook while you are pulling them in), along with recovering and landing of the fish.

An outstanding source for novices on all tackle-related things, fish species, equipment, tools and methods, is to be discovered in The Dorling Kindersley Encyclopedia of Fishing: The complete guide to the fish, tackle and techniques of fresh and saltwater angling. My intention and objective here is not to reiterate the noted facts discovered here. Devoted and avid anglers are readers and want the knowledge that is going to boost their chances of success. This source I suggest for old and young! (There are additionally certain other references noted by the end of this text, if you pick to pursue additional facts and/or long for deeper insights into the Bass fishing science and art).

All I am going to state is that having costly or the appropriate tools is not a guarantee that you are going to hook the next huge one! There are no actual guarantees in fishing. This is an activity in between nature and you . Exploring and reaching the point where you understand the function, feel and ingrained strengths and disadvantages of your tools, is the genuine way to wisdom. For many trial and error, perseverance and practice are the paths to follow to turn into skilled anglers with experience.

Understanding the tool's complete potential is going to require practice and time. Remember, that sophistication in tools is going to establish in parallel to your own proficiency and refinement of skill.

Your desired fishing style (from shore or boat, deep or shallow) is going to determine the most suitable option for tackle (rod and reel, line--density and weight), hooks, line, lures and baits, sinkers, weights, leaders and more.

Whether you are a salt-water enthusiast who delights in coast, boat, beach, or big-game fishing or a freshwater expert favoring bait, pole, lure and/or fly fishing, there are reels, rods, hooks, lines, leaders, baits, links, and landing tackles perfect for you.

Fundamental angling methods are fairly simple to master, yet conquering and fine-tuning all the subtleties and complex maneuvers and moves, looking into the tricks (found or yet to be uncovered), of bass fishing (which has a lot of versions and settings), is going to take a lifetime of enjoyment and defeat!

Practice and take pleasure in bass fishing, based upon your own style and niche, preference and place. It is a really individualized and personalized pursuit and enthusiasm. Constantly keep in mind, that there is a broad selection of enjoyment and variety available, by various types of fishing places, baits and lures, and so on, to keep angling intriguing and a growing sport. It is infectious and prevalent. As soon as you are in, it is tough to let go! You are hooked and being drawn in by this sport and pastime before you know it.

For many anglers, method (and choice of tools) is determined by the species looked for, established practice, conditions and more. Mainly synthetic lures are recommended and accepted for freshwater predatory fishing. Certain people choose live bait; others succeed with tough baits such as plastic worms and artificial rats.

Whether you are fishing from the boat, banks or float tube, the majority of people would recommend that you utilize a 6 to 6 and a half foot (1.8 -2 m) heavy-push-button, medium, bait-casting or spinning rod and reel mix, with powerful line (10-pound). In case you are fishing in heavy cover, weeds, slop, thick, swamps, grassy wetlands, and so on, a heavier line (braided) is going to serve you better/best. Hook sizes usually suggested are around a # 4 live-bait hook, honed and turned up somewhat (say around 10%). This is done to guarantee that the fish remained "hooked" and provides you a sporting opportunity to reel it in and land it effectively. A weed-less, # 5 hook can additionally serve you good in these conditions. Large-mouth bass could be captured at any depth, utilizing live baits throughout the majority of the year! Sharp hooks are the trick.

Sinkers and weights are another aspect you need to think about, particularly in cloudy, dark waters and/or when fishing in deep water particularly. There are additionally specialized sinkers, with rattles nowadays to attract the fish much more. They are really sensitive to noises, sound and water vibrations, so anything you could do to produce that appeal, tease and the temptation is fantastic to remember. Do whatever you can to activate their feeding response and guarantee a bite/strike!

Additionally, keep in mind, fish are a great deal like us-- on humid, hot days, they search for food, shelter and convenience. These are their feeding grounds (no different from us, wishing to sit beneath an umbrella, or before the TV, in a cool, air-conditioned area, attempting to remain cool and delight in our snacks).

Understanding and thinking about these habits is going to assist you in capturing additional fish. Search for the lily pads providing shade from the sun. Discover the ideal structure, depth and hide-away (they typically search for cover, as any other predator).

Shallow, weedy bays, rocks, hard-bottom flats, trees and/or other creeks, structures, deeper waters, channels, bluffs, drops, and more could all be part of their moving habitat and patterns, where they try to find food. They additionally enjoy being near the access point to deeper water. More later on their favored areas and how you can maximize these patterns.

Instances of luring methods and how the appropriate tools can assist you:

Top-water, Surface and/or Buzz baits: Acting nearly as a spinnerbait, yet with a flat blade that allows it to surface fast, this is a prominent selection for lots of bass aficionados. It draws in the bass, by producing a disruption along the surface like a minnow, activating their feeding impulses and predatory impulse to attack. Awarding you with an impressive catch!

Carolina Rig: this could quickly be referred to as just a variation of the standard, so-called 'Texas Rig' (see beneath), terrific for utilization with plastic worms or other soft bait. The majority of professional bass anglers recommend utilizing a heavier weight such as 1/2 -1 oz or more. Place the weight onto the line, follow with 3 plastic beads, a leader line, and a barrel swivel. What this enables the bass angler to do is to get the bait to 'fall' to the floor quickly and is particularly suggested for fishing deep waters.

The motion of the leader enables the bait to rise and swim over the bottom, and fall gradually down. For the majority of novices, this is simple to practice and do and is really flexible to get your regular tackle and rigging abilities to improve.

Crankbait: mainly describes lures, which are generally created from a range of materials, featuring tough wood or plastic. With an included feature of a diving lip on the front (simulating the motions of wobbling, natural prey, swimming and diving actions successfully), lures the bass to strike. The general rule, generally is that the bigger the lip, the deeper it is able to dive. Enhancements such as rattles are additionally helpful for particular conditions.

Jerk baits: An experienced favorite with bass anglers, for top-water, along with suspended bass fishing. Longer minnow-shaped plugs, available in a great deal of various colors and sizes. As a top-water, surface bait with a minor twitch-and-stop kind of retrieve, or perhaps as a more steady-and-slow retrieves underwater.

Another choice is to utilize suspending jerk baits which generally dive deeper, jerking it, nearly teasing and luring the bass to come up and bite.

Jigs: Certain people have illustrated these tackle as 'lead head and hook with dressing.' Their 'included' features might take the form of plastic or rubber skirts, soft plastic baits for bodies, rather than skirts. The majority of bass specialists integrate them with plastic bait or a frog as a follower (crawfish, plastic worm).

Lipless Crankbait: mainly describing sinking-type lures, created from plastic, in some cases with numerous rattles within for vibrations, noise, and causing disruptions beneath water.

Poppers: Topwater lures which carry a long-range punch. Retrieve with these types of lures are quick, jerky or move in one area for the entire duration. It could be rather helpful if you are attempting to find out where are the fish.

Soft Jerk bait: these could be utilized for an excellent impact similarly as a routine jerk bait, yet could be dropped to the bottom rather effectively too to tease out the bass, looking around for feast and food.

Spinnerbaits: an additional simulator of motion and prey on the go. It is really comparable to a jig, yet with a blade which goes over the hook, and spins to mimic a bass favorite too: fish.

Texas Rig: this is considered and called particularly for basic rigging with a plastic worm. Utilize a sliding weight, typically in shape of a bullet, and a hook adequate for the worm size you have selected. Hone the hook and jab the hook point straight into the head of the worm, bring it out the side approximately 1/8 - 3/16" beneath the entry, thread it once more. Turn the hook around, so that the point is encountering the body of the worm. Lay it over the side to see where it ought to go in order to hang directly. Place the work directly onto the hook if it is hanging. KEEP IN MIND: In case the worm is twisted, your action and line are going to pay the price and it is going to be less useful.

Walking-the-dog: this is an angling method that typically needs a bit of time to master, however, novices should not avoid trying it, for it is rather effective with bass. Casting over a reasonably long distance, enable the bait to sit for a short time period, take up the slack, and with your rod tip pointed at the water, give it a jerk to the side, then instantly move it backwards and draw in any slack, then jerk once again, and redo that all the way back.

You are, basically mimicking the prey's evasive movements, tempting the hunter to stalk, follow and strike! This may be your trump card.

Slip-bobbers, equipped with a 1/4 ounce plastic jig, live bait as a minnow, leech or nightcrawler at its tip and naturally, all on a hook that is sharpened.

Lightly shaking, jiggling, presenting this near any emerging brush or weeds, trees, underwater logs, cover or stumps, might prove effective.

Bear in mind that fish are continuously moving while feeding. The time of day, amount of sunshine, water temperature, and more all factor into the angling formula.

Bobber jigs or rigs are prominent and rather effective too. Slip-sinkers, Carolina (drop-shot rig) work effectively as well.

Free-line fishing in shallow waters might lead to good things. Casting a plain hook with live bait and feed the line to the bait, enabling it to 'swim' normally is going to draw in some attention.

Other professionals would suggest in case you are in the so-called watery salad, heavy slop or weeds, to go heavier. 20 lb line the minimum and sturdy, heavy-action, bait-casting reel and rod combinations with straight, lengthy handles to offer you leverage.

Drifting jig-heads, with a slip sinker rig, with 2-3 foot leader have shown to be valuable as well, particularly when kept near the bottom, watching not to get snagged while doing so. Weed-less hooks could aid you in recovering live-bait and/or hooked fish via extremely dense underbrush.

Once again, comprehending what bass, in fact, eat, when and where, is going to assist you with picking and presenting the most useful, suitable and appealing bait (whether live or synthetic). Making use of the natural fish diet, could help you in improving your lures and baits look, technique, tactics and ultimate success.

Bass, as a predator, is going to be trying to find specific colors, shapes and familiar movements. Plastic crawfish and worms are prominent options. Part of the reason bass is such a prominent species for fishing, is they are infamous for striking hard, biting powerfully and pulling strong -- a strong game fish for sure.

Spoons or spinners are synthetic baits which are particularly created for the purpose of enticing the fish. It is supposed to prompt, make a strike alluring, using the fish's natural impulse to feed and/or protect. It maximizes your odds of securing strikes. Rotation, skirts, color, fluttering action all work in conjunction to mimic motion and take advantage of the move.

Spoons move/act in a fishlike way in the water, trolled behind boats they are usually really effective and could additionally be cast and recovered. Plugs are created of numerous materials, created particularly to float, sink when reeling them in or back, or dive beneath the surface . They mimic surface disruption and lure fish with propellers or plastic skirts which flutter and move in the water.

Synthetic lures could be used alone or in the mix with natural or live baits. The size and kind of lure are going to depend upon the species, place and design of fishing you choose or pick to go after. (For instance spinning, trolling, and fly-fishing).

For bass fishing, especially, a handful of recommendations are to keep in mind that luring the predators from beneath takes competency, patience and practice. For matted weed-beds and careless pitches, you may need to tickle the surface a little. Whenever fishing in shallow waters, lures cast out quickly and recovered gradually, shaking it along, may set off a reaction. It is all in the tease and guarantees to the fish that search for indications of motion in the water.

Having an useful set of Polaroid sunglasses is a necessity! Continue moving the bait around and have fun with the presentation-- it is an art, obtained skill that improves gradually. When casting the bait out, attempt not to startle the fish, bearing in mind that they don't react well to noise/sound, motion and vibrations.

Plastic worms work effectively (around 10"). Being versatile, changing baits, different color, and so on, utilizing a good Texas rig, for instance, attaching a worm close to the hook bottom, moving it onto the shank, popping it through, with a 1/2 ounce weight may be all you require!

Having a 2nd rod established and prepared or fishing with a pal who can assist you in reacting rapidly (as the fish are constantly on the move) and when they are prepared to strike, you are ready for them! Others recommend utilizing braided line which is more powerful than mono (for when fishing in weedy locations), without any stretch that can lessen entanglement and maximize your odds of retrieval via thick cover and weeds.

Stiff rods which is able to endure the "fight" bass can normally put up are additional base-requirement for bass fishing aficionados. Shielding your rods with rod wraps, to minimize scrapes and dings could additionally maximize not just its performance, but keep your angling equipment in prime condition! Popping and shaking along lures/bait, develops a scenario that allows the fish to believe the "prey" is escaping.

Nevertheless, the appropriate tools, hooks, bait and place are insufficient! Some fundamental angling methods are needed, establishing your reel and rod, understanding the fundamentals about connecting knots for joining the line to tackle, forming loops and more.

Connecting a secure knot is the main point here, as each one of them might present a 'weak point,' which you do not want when the bass is hooked! Some recommend before tightening up a knot, to damp it with a bit of water and cut all loose ends and edges, to prevent drag/snag.

Tube-jigs, gulp-tubes whih are scented, are other choices. The chewy, soft substance fools the fish into not wishing to let go and have another chew, therefore boosting your chances of landing it securely.

Top-water baits with rattles are also fairly prominent, with slack in the line, walking-the-dog (flipping) produces an appealing show for the fish.

Having a spinner-bait with a bit of red in it mimics blood or injured prey to our underwater predator, activating yet again their natural impulses and feeding reaction, boosting your chances of getting a bite, strike or hit.

Whether you end up in a flat-bottom bass boat or a jet-boat, coast, rocks, cliff, beach, lake, river, reservoir, or other water surface, sturdy rods, hot hands, great tackle, proper preparation, the appropriate presentation and bait, precise casting, where you understand the fish may move/be/feed naturally, fishing for pattern and structure, having an eye on surroundings and circumstances, could all make those short-lived moments of elation and anticipation initially strike momentous!

The fights, flights, turns, flips and leaps, attacks and tough hits, battles, retrieval and bass landing, is what keeps us returning!

Let us now have a look at what other considerations, angling methods, tricks, blunders and specialty situations could teach us about the pleasurable activity and art, which is bass fishing!

Environmental Factors

As pointed out during this text up until now, there are numerous elements that we frequently do rule out, and/or dismiss when we initially begin angling for bass. These would involve consideration of:

Water stratification and depths (bass are discovered at differing levels and understanding where (at what level), to fish for them is critical); deep or shallow, in some cases both.

As far as water temperatures go, throughout a seasonal/yearly cycle, waters turn, move and become re-oxygenized. As temperature levels fall, from deep beneath and throughout ice forms, streams to the surface, liquefies and moves down once again. Science has actually supplied us with sufficient proof that 3 layers form in a body of water-- such as a lake, for instance. Colder/deeper, Milder/middle-ground, transitional layer and the surface/top/warmer waters.

Heeding these levels and differing temperature levels and oxygen-rich areas are all aspects to think about even prior to going out. Think the procedure through. Think as the fish would-- ask yourself, where would you go, in all probability, if you were confronted with the identical circumstance-- the response is going to primarily lead you to where the fish more than probably are!

A depth meter and a temperature gauge could all prepare you more, as an angler, well-informed and ready, to evaluate the environment, better comprehend it, gain from it, and utilize the information you collect and handy, to KNOW or ideally judge, where the fish are going to be at!

Depth is a terrific sign of what the bass are after and where they are going to be probably discovered. This is going to determine your tackle, approach and how you perform your angling abilities to landthe bass! In case you fish at the appropriate level, comprehending why the fish are there, on the move, feeding, and so on, you are going to boost your chances significantly of getting strikes and hooking your following huge catch. It may even be a trophy! The depth is connected to the optimal comfort zone of the bass and the temperature level. Constantly ask yourself what they would choose on a day such as today and after that, go fish there. Measure with temperature, depth-sensing units, GPS, and so on, to determine the depth and pattern of the day.

Temperature

The majority of bass species favor a temperate climate-- their metabolic process is affected, if not governed practically by the waters they are in. They can additionally endure quite a vast array of temperatures; for that reason, we can fish basically during the year. (60- 75 degrees Fahrenheit)/ It is additionally less commonly understood that ice-fishermen hook bass in deeper waters, at approximately 33-39.1 degree water temperatures! When it become get cooler, they get rather slower, as their environment cools off substantially, and having this in mind is going to yield and enhance your catch.

Oxygen is additionally really crucial to fish. The hotter it becomes, the closer they are going to remain to coast and to plant-life, which generates oxygen and/or where they may catch the occasional breeze. Reading these signals nature offers right, is going to make any angler better to go where the fish are and hook the bass. Additionally search for areas which aren't too stagnant and filled with rotting plants, as this may be an oxygen-deprived location with not a big fish concentration, they have to 'breathe' to survive as well!

Water Condition

Clear and/or dirty-- you are going to discover bass in both! Their mode of attack and behavior are going to alter as they strategize how to ideally expend their energies in the survival, hunt for food, and so on. Predators by nature, prefer deeper waters, structure and cover. When spawning, or on really hot days, you are going to probably discover them more in the shallows.

Bass constantly have a 'back-door' access to deeper waters. These truths ought to be able to point you in the basic vicinity of where the fish are rather aptly. The male bass is additionally extremely protective of the spawn site/nest and is going to protect it, strike at any identified danger or trespasser. Fishing is no more left up to random, reflective, ruminative trial and error casting.

Now, today, substituted with more a more focused, driven, thought-through, analytical and justified competitive approach, that attempts to comprehend patterns, habits, conditions, environment, season and so on sometimes depending on the help of technology and tools to help and improve your odds of identifying, finding, hooking, recovering and landing the fish effectively (primarily in deeper waters!). For that reason, if the waters are clear, go for deeper waters as a basic guideline.

Noise/Vibrations/Disturbances

DO NOT DISTURB signs are tough to place in the water! Constantly keep in mind that there is a bit of truth to not scaring the fish away and being rather cautious and peaceful around them. The bass specifically utilizes its entire body as a sounding board. Any surface disruption, water displacement or movement is going to attract their attention-- this could actually aid and/or harm your angling dreams and hopes.

Squeaky, rusty oars, loud motors and even the noise of a quick, far cast might interfere and/or get their attention. Understanding any, motion, identifying fish in their environment, things (plants, water) moving around, could be great indications. Wearing a great Polaroid sunglasses pair might additionally assist you to see more in the intense sunshine and glare, and water reflections.

Color, Time of day, Sunlight

A lot of bass anglers say that dusk and dawn are the best feeding time for the bass-- not the height of day or when the sun is at its brightest and the water might be a level or more too hot for our fishy buddies and when they go for cover and/or depths. It is a concern of enticing their natural impulses.

They are eager observers and motion and color have actually been examined in the bass species. Choosing a lure that resembles their prey is going to optimize your odds of capturing more bass. This does not indicate that they are not going to strike during the night, for instance, or at other times throughout the day-- you may simply need to adjust and utilize some expert methods to draw them out a little!

Time of Year

Weather, surroundings and angling guidelines change. The players and stage do not stay the exact same and even on the identical day, daily, things are going to differ. This variety (the spice of life most say) is what keeps the majority of us thinking, adjusting, changing approach, depth, bait, and so on, all in the continued pursuit and hope of capturing the bass.

Regarding the best time to capture bass-- viewpoints differ significantly on this subject. In some locations, fishing is just enabled after spawning. Summer, spring and fall (with fall being the ideal for a lot of larger fish) and even winter some kind of bass fishing is available to you, based upon where you are, what the weather conditions are like and what kind of year the bass are having (condition of the water they reside and flourish in, spawning success, stocking, the eco-system, pollution and so on). Even ice fishing is feasible.

As mentioned previously, weather impacts habits and the season and kind of water may all necessitate various methods, tools and bait and preparation/lures and presentation.

As an angler, devoted bass angler, this is not going to faze you whatsoever! On the contrary, it supplies you with the chance to move gears, alter your approach, tools, fine-tune abilities, and discover more about your prey and its practices. By being alert, mindful and watchful, you are going to discover a great deal about the fish-- it is no more a passive sport! High air pressure, water movement, choppy waves, cloudy skies, masking of the sun, all might determine whether fish are going to be biting or not. Color of plastic worms might be changed from blue (on bright days) to black (on cloudy days without a great deal of sun). Customizing your fishing methods and adjusting to patterns of the weather, even adapting your lures/bait, are all techniques of the bass master!

Bass are additionally sensitive to really bright sunshine, so then you may discover them searching for a bit of shady cover and/or cooler waters. That understanding is going to prepare you good for where to be and search for them, boosting your chances of discovering them as well!

Predatory Nature

They are rather predictable. As hunters, they do particular things, intuitively, and as anglers, we take advantage of it. There are great deals of truths about the types, worth understanding. Thinking as a hunter ourselves and sometimes as the fish, can boost your chances and success considerably. Being one with nature and its patterns, habits, quirkiness and balance, enable anglers to be competent, accurate, ready and more effective, instead of leaving it up to probability and randomness.

Favorite habitat

One author likens topographic maps and contour to bass fishermen, such as treasure maps to pirates were once. Lines reveal depth, elevation, and so on. Learn what the bottom or floor of the water would appear like, it is hardly ever flat, typically characterized by humps and rises, drop-offs and slopes.

Access-points into deeper water and slopes ought to additionally yield more regular, bigger hauls and additional strikes, as bass choose to have access to deeper waters and are continuously moving, searching and feeding and/or protecting territory.

Natural Diet

The art of luring fish: producing the appropriate conditions/ allure/atmosphere for a strike.

Lots of things have already been stated about this subject.

Confidence

The belief in your capability to find and capture the numerous bass species is, without a doubt, the ideal tool of the trade to cultivate and develop in time. This could not be bought and is a call to each angler, to feature in his/her tackle-box!

Whether you select to utilize spinners, or swear by crawfish, plastic worms and other bait, chum or have a preferred lure for reasons and/or secret tricks, you utilize what works ideally and what you think is going to lead to the bass you desire, want and need to have! A positive mindset goes far when finding out how to catch bass. By benefiting from continuous experience, failure and success, your angling and chances are going to keep improving. Practicing, in this instance, is going to go a long way to allow for success in this unforeseeable, differing scenario-- when you are individually with the most well-known sporting fish and game of them all.

Bass Fishing Tricks

Precise Casting

Mastering fundamental casting is crucial. A lot of bait-casting and spinning rod and reel mixes today, are produced for hassle-free, ease-of-use versatility by a range of anglers (multi-level at that as well!).

Make an effort to get rid of errors from your overall style and method. Capability and precision ought to matter more than power and it is not constantly about getting it as far out, as quick as you potentially could (even though this might be essential in particular scenarios and situations as well!).

Casting, getting your hook/bait/line, weights, sinkers, and leaders in and into the water, at the precise right depth, mimicking 'prey', and doing so with severe, pinpoint precision, is what this is about. Striking your target with self-confidence is a really fundamental ability to master and fine-tune. Getting the hook out to precisely where you desired it to be is what you need to work for and practice.

Casting is one component of this procedure, getting the lure to the appropriate depth quite another. Advanced bass anglers recommend utilizing a counting or countdown technique. Rather easy actually. From the second the bait strikes the water, begin counting, 1000, 1000 and 1, 1000 and 2, 1000 and 3 ... approximating the seconds it is going to require for it to drop into the water. This is going to assist you in understanding much better what you are doing. When it strikes the bottom, for instance. Whether it got caught on something while doing so and so on. You develop reference points in and on the water.

Rod in-hand, and hands-on is the ideal way. Practice-plugs in your own backyard, or in the park is going to make you that more successful and precise, on and in the water, regardless of the body of water, or fishing style you pick. Whether spinning, fly-rodding or baitcasting, there is a thing for each taste. Even missed targets, failures and tries, are likewise great teachers, as this method is something of a routine you could understand and master.

Casting a lure with a spinning reel, bait casting and casting float and/or leger rig are extremely comparable. Lure fishing, floating, spinning, plugs, spoons, top-water or surface lures, , trolling, crankbait, and so on, are all standard methods which need exposure, fast demonstrations and hands-on practice. I recommend a DVD or video, or thorough online explanation, seeing a fishing program and getting guidelines from others and specialists, in addition to finding and specifying your own style you are comfy and prosperous with. The appeal of bass fishing is that it provides something for everybody, regardless of your previous fishing experience!

Concentrating on your grip, spinning reels, bait-casters, and/or closed-face spin casters approaches and mastery, selecting a target, striving to land your lure in the center of that target, is an excellent strategy.

As a basic guideline, a great arch in the air as a travel path is a great goal and reference to have, as you set out to enhance your casting method and precision. Line-control is essential to stay clear of overshooting, achieve a gentler landing, sluggish flight (by touching the the spool lip with the tip of your forefinger (additionally referred to as 'feathering') is very helpful.

Landing Fish

Knowing how a fish feels on your hook, rod and line is extremely essential. Retrieval has to do with more than just getting the fish into the eager hands/boat/net. Proficiency, responsiveness, maneuvering, tackle understanding, reel-clutching, well-balanced control, fighting curves and bending/arching rods and the different settings and controls, methods (consisting of hooking, playing, casting, reeling in, recovering and landing is necessary. They are a lot more than simple steps in the procedure and/or sum-total of parts.

To interpret it as a real blue-blood bass-fishing experience, appreciation of the symphony of the interaction of procedure and result, tactics, methods, angler, tools, the catch and haul is what is important here. When utilizing a bait-casting/spinning reel, there are 3 crucial methods to master which would entail reel control: with anti-reverse on, back winding (anti-reverse off) and thumb-pressure control.

There is absolutely nothing more amazing than a fish on the run. Apply pressure, keep the rod up a little and boost the drag if needed, utilizing one of the methods above. Keep an eye on tension and stay away from line-breaks and let the fish get tired.

It is one thing to get ready, tease, cast, and lure, hook and ultimately reel in. The procedure, nevertheless, does not stop there. More of the mastery of standard methods consists of techniques of landing fish, such as beaching (not appropriate for catch and release), tailing (not fit for every species), lipping (see the teethed species here!), netting or perhaps gaffing (prohibited in a lot of locations, because of the danger of the strike hurting the fish).

The most helpful suggestion I can offer or recommend is staying in control, not to upset or surprise the fish additionally. Enable the exhausted fish to turn, submerge the net and not lunge at it.

During lipping, grip the lower lip carefully between your forefingers and thumb, unhook thoroughly or keep in the water while releasing it carefully, yet effectively, without injuring the fish, sticking as far as you can, to present and approved, and catch-and-release routines.

Lure-Fishing and Spinning

Spinning tackle and synthetic lures and baits are going up in popularity and the most well-known type of fishing across the world. As far as bass fishing goes, one of the simplest ways to draw in the species-- even for beginner and novice anglers of any fishing style and age and skill-levels. Rotation, color and motion, remaining as true as you are able to the natural target prey and diet of the bass is going to maximize your odds. The density and shape of the spinning 'blade' on the lure impacts the mobility and action of the lure-- how it acts and reacts in and beneath water.

Floating lures are additionally popular and helpful specifically for deep-water bass fishing. Look for snagging at the bottom and make sure to weigh it properly utilizing appropriate weights. This approach guarantees getting the bait at the eye-level of the fish.

For spoons, there are 2 broad classifications, specifically casting and trolling spoons. Weedless lures primarily have hooks with metal or nylon weed-guards that protect against snagging and/or non-weedless spoons are additionally frequently utilized. How to tell which one to utilize, a lot of bass anglers try to find weight, speed and shape. The ideal way to find your way around in any tackle box or store is to practice and learn more about the habits and/or success in various conditions. Attempt to learn more about the optimal retrieval and success rates, perhaps even jotting it down in your journal as you tackle your bass hunt/journey.

Plugs, surface lures, beneficial at all speeds, at all fishing levels, make these lures flexible, nimble and an all-time favorite of plenty of a bass anglers. Match the lure to the conditions you deal with and the situation, body of water and particular species you are after (large-mouth, small-mouth, spotted, striped, yellow, rock, black, white, and so on). Shallow-diving crank-bait and/or top-water or surface lures have actually shown to be the most helpful for bass fishing-- excellent for fishing shallows. Stick-baits and jerking, prop-baits, minnow plugs, crawler-type top-water baits, surface disturbers, and even a driving, floating crank-bait could prove beneficial.

The true trick is in what some refer to as the 'one-two punch, luring and teasing with a teaser or top-water, and after that, using a plastic worm, for instance, on a 2nd rod, for maximizing strikes, and tipping the scales in your favor once more.

Plastic Worms

There is a vast selection of worms offered on the marketplace (both live bait and synthetic). For passionate bass anglers, they are a requirement. The method to master is hooking them correctly. When hooking a worm, it is vital to make sure that you thread it effectively. Get a great deal of the body onto the hook, hooking it two times, at bottom and top. This is to make sure that it does not fly loose as you are casting it within the water. It additionally shields it to some degree in the submerged heaven which the bass shares with other fish, who may wish to come and take a sample or bite! Utilizing worms in mix with other lures/baits and luring techniques such as hard-bait and/or top-water surface disturbers or eels, frogs, or whatever species and body of water would consider suitable "feeding prey" for the bass of your preference and selection is the secret. Again adjusting your approach when needed and offering the bass a range of foods to pick from, are all ideally going to improve your chances.

Chapter 2 - Mistakes and Tricks

As we have actually uncovered during these pages, there is a lot to bass fishing. As soon as you are familiar with the species, various bodies of water, various and advanced fishing and angling tools and add-ons, along with acquainting yourself with routines, nature and patterns, habits, natural diet and favored foods, mastering some fundamental abilities such as presentation, preparation, bait, tackle and lures, casting precision, hooks, knots and the complexities and intricacies in landing and retrieval, the journey has began. There is a lot more to check out and discover through the adventure, art, sport and competitive science which is bass fishing.

Even though, there are certain final thoughts I can provide on a few of the more frequent casting missteps. All these 'mistakes' are present in the current literature and might quickly be overcome to maximize your bass fishing haul and experience. Here are but a couple of problems most novices have an issue with:

1. Overshot lure with excessive power in the preliminary cast and the line release not slowed

2. The lure being too light or falling short, with the line being launched prematurely throughout the cast and/or the rod being too high after the line being launched.

3. Lure landing too roughly, because of the launch at the angle which is too low and not arching sufficiently in the air.

4. Imprecise casting (the most frequent)-- missing the mark, when the lure gets off-course with excessive side-to-side motioning/action during casting. Practicing reel and line command, along with the overhead cast may assist.

Great deal of texts (such as the Dorling Encyclopedia), advise thinking of casting, such as the motion of the clock- face arms, starting in the two o'clock position, going back to about the noon- position and back to the 2 once more, with the rod somewhat lowered as the lure falls deeper within the water. For the majority of novices, this 'visualization' typically aids to fine-tune technique.

Chapter 3 - Bass Fishing Styles

Skipping

This method may remind you a lot of tossing rocks onto the water surface to see it skip. As a top-water/water disruption and motion simulator, it teases and triggers the bass to come up and see what is there to attack/eat.

Spinning reel and rods combo are ideal for fishing and reaching bass where they swim and conceal beneath docks, piers and pontoons. Additionally helpful for getting beneath and into growth and underbrush. Remember their 'comfort zone.' On bright days, bass search for food, shade and shelter and frequently rest here in shady places, beneath structure cover.

Ripping

Some call this the toss it out, jerk, twitch and go technique. A medium-action rod with action and parabolic bend. It may, in fact, deceive our bass-friend into believing there is an 'injured' prey around. As a professional, allow the worm to drop and sink to the bottom, staying there for some time. Reel some slack out of the line, grabbing the worm with a sharp, long rod tip upsweep. Let 'er rip! Let it sink down once again to the bottom, while gradually bringing down the rod tip-- continue mimicking live prey as this, swimming, moving and bobbing about and your predator is going to attack it with fury.

Drift Trolling

Trailing behind the boat, worms move and crawl covering the bottom, mimicking prey in its pure form. Lower and raise it sometimes, looking natural and appealing to any bass close by hunting for a yummy morsel.

Fly-Rodding

In rivers, ponds, lakes and streams, this method is rather helpful. Fly-fishing methods are extremely helpful with bass. Start by rigging and preparing a plastic worm, adding a little split-shot just before the hook. This is going to allow it to sink gradually. Cast or flip and enable it to bob and drop to the bottom. Quite the tease for the keen-sighted bass. Have the rod tip really low, to render it feasible for you to make a timely strike when you feel a bass hit.

Night and Ice-fishing

Schooling, successful dropping and tackle the bait/lure right before the fish, not having them use up a great deal of energy is the secret for these conditions and timings. Water has a tendency to be cooler and all your methods, techniques and strategies have to slow down a notch. Bass additionally have a tendency to school, throughout these times. Understanding this truth can assist you in getting your target more and boosting your chances of getting a hit under these uncommon or specialized conditions.

It is practically an impossibility here to deal with each distinct condition and we hardly scratched the surface on the majority of the contexts bass anglers may be in.

Conclusion

Catch-and-Release

Doing your part to keep nature safe and save it for upcoming generations, is regulated and mandatory. Utilizing barbless hooks and/or extracting them quickly. Holding the fish in the water carefully while unhooking, lessening the damage and trauma to the fish is vital. Support the fish and release it with the present, so it can swim away and live another day.

Do all you are able to to comprehend and stick to permits, closed season terms, licensing, size and catch restrictions. These and other measures exist to serve and protect, to lessen the threat of over-fishing and species ending up being extinct.

This may not be the supreme book on bass fishing ever made, yet might the contents and passion motivate you to success as a devoted and effective angler. If I can fire up self-confidence and hints of exhilaration for fisher-people, old and young, then these pages have actually done well!

May the delights of Bass fishing and the numerous manners in which we are able to select actively to take part in it, bring you constant and continuous pleasure, haul, reward, and tremendous enjoyment!

Glossary

Action - Measure of rod effectiveness that illustrates the time between flexion and going back to straight setup; goes from slow to quick, with slow being the biggest amount of flexion; additionally describes the rod durability (heavy, medium and light) with heavy being a stout rod and light a limber rod; additionally describes gear of reels.

Active Fish - Bass which are striking boldly and feeding greatly.

Adaptation - Biological modification which boosts fitness.

Algae - Basic plant organisms.

Alkalinity - Measurement of the quantity of bases that neutralize acids.

Alley - An opening between spots of emerging weeds; additionally the parallel area splitting emerging weeds and the coastline.

Amp - Measure of electrical current.

Amp Hour - Measure of a deep-cycle battery storage capability acquired by multiplying the current circulation in amps with the hours that it is created.

Angler - Individual utilizing rod or pole and reel to capture fish.

Anti-reverse - System that stops the reels from spinning reversely.

Backlash – Line tangle on a bait-casting reel because of spool overrun.

Backwater - Shallow river area.

Bag Limit - Limitation on the amount of fish an angler might acquire within a day.

Bail – Semicircular, metal arm on a spinning reel (open-face) which, after a cast, engages the line.

Bait - A synthetic lure is generally what is implied despite the fact that bait can additionally indicate live bait.

Baitcasting - Fishing with a baitcasting rod and a revolving-spool reel; reel installed on the rod topside.

Baitfish - Little fish frequently consumed by predators.

Bar – Long water ridge.

Basic Requirements - Describes the 3 survival requirements of bass: , safery, reproduction, and food.

Bay - Significant imprint on the coastline of a reservoir or lake.

Bite - When a fish touches or takes a bait to ensure that the angler feels it. Additionally called a bump, hit or a strike.

Black Bass - Typical term utilized to explain numerous kinds of bass, such as the smallmouth, largemouth and spotted bass.

Blank - Fishing pole without grip, finish or guides.

Brackish - Water of medium salinity between freshwater and seawater.

Break - Distinct variation in otherwise continuous stretches of structure, cover or bottom type. Generally anything, that "separates" the terrain underwater.

Break line - A line of sudden shift in bottom type, depth or water clearness in the feature of typically consistent structure. A location where there is an unexpected or extreme shift in the weed type or water depth. This might be a submerged cliff, the creek edge, or perhaps a stand of submerged weeds.

Brush line - The interior or the exterior edge of a brush stretch.

Brush pile - Typically describes a mass of medium to small-sized tree limbs within the water. Brush piles might be only one or two feet in length, or they might be very big and they might be submerged or noticeable. They could be manmade or produced by Nature. They typically hold fish. And anglers.

Bumping - Describes making a lure hit a thing like a tree, log or pier piling in a measured way. This is frequently done inadvertently but coul get the identical response from the fish.

Buzzbait - Topwater bait with big, propeller-type blades that churn the water throughout the retrieve. Made up of a leadhead, stiff hook, and wire that supports several blades.

Buzzing - Recovering a lure, like a buzzbait or spinnerbait, at a rate quick enough to trigger it to stay partly out of the water, triggering a loud disruption. Often called burning or ripping.

Cabbage - Any of numerous types of weeds, situated underwater or over the surface, of the genus Potamogeton.

Carolina Rig - A terminal tackle style typically utilized to keep a lure a foot or two from the bottom. This is most typically utilized with a plastic worm, yet is additionally utilized with floating crankbaits and other lures too. A barrel slip sinker of 1/2- to 1-ounce is initially placed on the line, and after that, a swivel is connected to the line end. A bit of line 18 to 30 inches long is then connected to the other swivel end, and a lure or hook is connected to this piece line end. Rigged Texas-style (weedless with the hook buried in the bait body), the mix is outstanding for fishing ledges, sandbars, humps and points.

Channel - The bed of a river or stream.

Chugger - Topwater plug with a head that is dished-out created to create a splash when yanked forcefully.

Clarity - Describes the depth at which you are in a position to observe an item (like your lure) beneath the water.

Cold Front - A weather condition alonged by clear, high skies, and an unexpected decrease in temperature level.

Contact Point - The deepest place on a structure where a bass angler could initially successfully show his lure to bass as they move from deep water.

Controlled Drift - The act of utilizing a drift sock, an electrical motor or oars to let drift to be achieved at a specific direction/speed. This term is typically referred to as "drift fishing" by many anglers.

Coontail - Submerged hornwort family aquatic plant usually discovered in hard water; identified by forked, stiff leaves.

Cosmic Clock - The sun's seasonal impact on weather conditions and water relating to wind, barometric pressure, and cloud cover.

Count It Down - Timing a sinking lure to identify when it is going to get to a defined depth. This is achieved by discovering the sinking rate of a lure in feet-per-second. Frequently utilized during fishing for suspended fish.

Cove - An imprint along a shoreline.

Cover - Manmade or natural things on the lake bottom, impoundments or rivers, specifically those that sway fish habits. Anything a fish can utilize to hide itself. Instances consist of tree lines, stick-ups, rocks, stumps, pilings, logs, weeds, docks, duck blinds, boathouses, bushes, and so on.

Crankbait - Normally, a lipped lure which dives beneath the surface throughout the retrieve. So-named lipless crankbaits are slim, minnow-like lures which sink at a speed of around 1-foot every second.

Dabbling - Working a lure down and up in the identical area a dozen or more times beside a tree or within a bush.

Depthfinder - A sonar gadget, either a flasher system or LCR recorder, utilized to read the bottom structure, identify depth, and sometimes, in fact, find the fish; additionally referred to as a fishfinder.

Disgorger - Device for getting rid of hooks deeply ingrained in the fish throat.

Drag - Device on fishing reels that lets the line to pay out beneath pressure, although the reel is engaged. When set properly, it assures versus line breakage.

Drop-Off - An abrupt boost in depth, developed by land points, gulley washes, little creek channels, and the basic layout.

Ecology - The biology branch handling the connection between organisms and their habitat.

Edge - Describes the borders developed by a structure/greenery change in a lake. Certain instances of edges are weed lines, tree lines, and the edge of a drop-off.

Euthrophic - Extremely fertile waters distinguished by shallow, warm basins.

Fan Cast - Making a series of casts just a couple of degrees apart to encompass a half-circle

Farm Pond - Little body of water that is manmade.

Feeder Creek - Tributary to a stream.

Feeding Times - Particular times during the day when fish are most active. These are connected with the the moon and sun position and are described as solunar tables (additionally called moon charts) and are foreseeable for any location and time.

Filamentous Algae - Kind of algae identified by long chains of connected cells that provide it a stringy look and feel.

Feeding Cycle - Specific regular periods throughout which bass satisfy their cravings.

Instances: Minor or Major Solunar durations; sunrise, sundown.

Finesse Fishing - An angling method defined by using light tackle - rods, line, reel and synthetic baits (typically grubs, tube worms, or other tiny soft-plastic lures); typically effective in clear, relatively tidy water.

Flat - A spot in water with little if any depth change. Little and big, flats are typically surrounded by deeper water on at least one side, the bottom comes up to create a flat location where fish are going to typically go up for feeding.

Flipping - The method of positioning a lure in a given area specifically, and silently, with as little disruption of the water as feasible utilizing an underhand cast while managing the line with your hand.

Flipping Stick - Heavy action fishing pole, 7 to 8 feet long, created for bass fishing.

Florida Rig - Extremely comparable to the Texas Rig, the only distinction is the fact that the weight is bound by screwing it into the bait.

Fly 'N Rind - Identical thing as jig-and-pig - a mix of a pork rind trailer and leadhead jig.

Forage - Little baitfish, crayfish and other animals which bass consume. Might additionally be utilized in the sense of the bass searching for something to eat.

Front - Weather system that results in modifications in cloud cover, temperature, rainfall, barometric pressure and wind.

Gear Ratio - Measure of a reels' retrieve velocity; the amount of times the spool revolves for every total handle turn.

Grayline - Grayline allows you to compare weak and strong echoes. It "paints" gray on targets that are more powerful than a predetermined value. This enables you to tell the distinction between a tough and soft bottom. For instance, a soft, weedy or muddy bottom returns a weaker symbol, that is shown with a slim or no gray line. A tough bottom returns a powerful signal, that leads to a broad gray line.

Grub - A brief plastic worm utilized with a weighted jig hook.

Habitat - The location in nature where an animal or plant species resides. The water, greenery, and all that comprises the lake, which is where bass reside. Habitat, for other animals, is additionally in the cities and woods, it's generally a term utilized to suggest a "living location" or home environment.

Hard Bottom - Location in a water body with a strong base - gravel, clay, sand, rock. The kind of bottom where you would not sink far, if whatsoever, were you to step on it.

Hawg - Typically describes a hefty bass weighing 4 pounds or more.

Holding Location - Structure that repeatedly holds 3 to 5 bass that can be caught.

Holding Station - Put on a lake where non-active fish devote the majority of their time.

Honey Hole - An great fishing area consisting of a variety of huge bass; likewise, any location with a big concentration of keeper bass.

Horizontal Motion - The distance a fish moves while staying at the identical depth.

Hump - A place higher than the surrounding location. A submerged dam or island may be taken into consideration as a hump.

Ichthyology - The zoology branch which handles fishes - their category, structure, routines, and life history.

Non-active Fish - Bass that remain in a non-feeding state of mind. Instances of usually inactive times: following a cold front; throughout a significant weather change that results in an abrupt increase or water temperature fall, or when an increasing lake level is quickly reduced.

Inside Bend - The inside line of a creek channel or a grass bed.

Isolated Structure - A possible holding area for bass; instances consist of a single bush on a point, a big tree that has actually fallen under the water, or a midlake hump.

Jig - A leadhead put around a hook and including a skirt of rubber, plastic, or hair.

Jig-N-Pig - Mix of a pork rind trailer and leadhead jig; amongst the most helpful baits for drawing in trophy-size bass.

Keeper - A bass which complies with a particular minimum length limitation developed by tournament companies and/or state fisheries department.

Lake Modification Sources - Components that alter bodies of water, like wave action, ice action, and erosion.

Lake Zones - Classification that consists of 4 classifications: open water, shallow water, basin and deep water.

Laydown - A tree which has actually fallen in the water.

Light Strength - The quantity of light which could be gauged at specific water depths; the higher the strength, the further down the light is going to project. This measurement could be considerably impacted by wind conditions and water clearness. In waters where light strength is low, vibrantly colored lures are wise options.

Line Guides - Rod rings for passing the fishing line.

Lipless Crankbaits - Synthetic baits created to look like a swimming baitfish. Such plugs wobble and/or vibrate throughout retrieve; some have integrated rattles. Likewise referred to as swimming baits.

Livewell - An oxygenated tank in boats utilized to keep fish in the water up until weigh-in time so that they have a greater survival possibility when launched. Comparable to an aquarium.

Logjam - A horizontal log group pressed together by water or wind circulation to form a blockage. In lakes, logjams are normally discovered near the coast and in the cove backs.

Loose-Action Plug - A lure with slow and wide, side to side motions.

Micropterus Salmoides - Scientific term for largemouth bass.

Migration Route - The course followed by bass when going from one location to another.

Milfoil - Surface-growing water plants.

Mono - Monofilament fishing line.

Moon Times - 4 stages of the moon are generally what the angler is interested in. Typically, the "ideal times" in a month take place 3 days prior and 3 days after, and consist of the day of the full or new moon. First-quarter and second-quarter durations are seen as just "good times."

Off Color - Describes the quality and/or color of the water. Brown is muddy due to rain runoff, black due to tannic acid and greenish due to algae.

Our Hole - Proprietary term utilized by anglers to define the location where they want to fish(My hole, their hole, and so on). Although, in fact, all holes are all angler's holes considering that the lakes for fishing are primarily public water. It's just your hole if you arrive initially. Otherwise, it's their hole.

Outside Bend - The exterior line of a grass bed or creek channel could be seen as an outside bend.

Oxbow - A river bend with a U-shape.

Pattern - A specified set of presentation and location elements that regularly produce fish. Instance: If you capture more than one fish off a stick-up or pier, then your odds of capturing more bass in such locations are exceptional. This is typically referred to as "establishing a pattern."

Pegging - Placing a toothpick in the slip sinker hole to stop the sinker from moving along the line. Other products like rubber bands slipped via the sinker have actually additionally ended up being prominent and don't snag line.

PFD – PFD means Personal Floatation Device; additionally referred to as a life vest.

pH - This is a measurement for fluids to figure out whether they are alkaline or acidic. On a scale between 1 and 10, 7 is taken into consideration as neutral. Beneath 7 the fluid is acidic and above 7 it is alkaline. This is an aspect which plays a part in the lake health and the fish in addition to where the fish might be discovered in a lake.

pH Meter - Just as a thermometer gauges cold and heat, a pH meter could be utilized to measure the level of alkalinity and acidity of water. The pH scale varies from 0 to 14. Bass usually choose water that is somewhat alkaline between 7.5 and 7.9. Water with a pH lower than 7 is acidic. Once prominent amongst significant bass anglers, the device is no longer commonly utilized.

Pick-Up - The action of a bass taking a gradually fished lure, like a crawfish, plastic worm or lizard.

Pit - Location dug up for mining operations which fills with water.

Pitching - Presentation method in which jigs or worms are dropped into cover at close proximity with an underhand pendulum movement, utilizing a 6 to 71/2 foot baitcasting rod. It is pitching of the bait beneath tree limbs or into a pocket. Comparable to flipping, however, it demands less stealth and is generally carried out from larger distances.

Pocket - A little imprint of the coastline.

Post Front - The duration after a cold front; atmosphere purifies itself and ends up being bright; generally identified by powerful winds and a substantial drop in temperature level.

Presentation - A collective term describing the selection of the kind of color, lure and size; structure targeted; the quantity of disruption a bait makes when getting in the water; and retrieval method, depth and speed utilized to capture fish. This describes the situations and manner (direction and speed, and so on) in which a lure is demonstrated to a fish.

Pro - A very few of the country's leading bass anglers can really claim the word pro. Not only should the pro be a constant cash winner on the major tournament circuits, yet he/she should additionally be articulate, an excellent salesman, provide a clean-cut image, and have the capability to show other people how to capture fish.

Professional Overrun - A respectful word for backlash.

Revolving-Spool Reel - A word for a baitcasting reel. The spool turns throughout the casting, as opposed to the spindle of a spincasting or spinning reel.

Reservoir - Synthetically developed location where water is gathered and kept; additionally referred to as an impoundment.

Riprap - A manufactured stretch of rocks or components of a difficult structure that typically extends over and beneath the coastline; typically discovered close to the dams of huge impoundments.

Saddle - A site where structure narrows prior to expanding once again.

Sanctuary - Deep-water home for bass.

Scatter Point - Place along the structure where bass begins to separate or spread; frequently discovered in shallow water, at or really near to a breakline.

Short Strike - When a fish strikes a lure and doesn't hit it.

Slack Line - The loose line from the lure to the rod top. This could be a minor line bow to an excess of line resting on the water.

Slicks - Bass not sufficiently long to fulfill tournament requirements; normally less than 14 inches. Such fish additionally are referred to as through backs, nubbins, babies, pop corns and dinks.

Slip Sinker - A lead weight with a hole through the middle. Threaded on line, a slip sinker slides easily backwards and forwards.

Slough - A narrow, long water stretch like a little stream or feeder tributary off a river or lake.

Slow Roll - Spinnerbait presentation wherein the lure is recovered gradually through and over cover items.

Slush Bait - Topwater plug with a pointed or flat head.

Spincaster - A way of fishing utilizing a closed-face spinning reel, push-button and baitcasting rod; reel is installed on the rod topside.

Spinnerbait - A leadhead lure comparable to an open safety-pin which has a hook; other features consist of plastics, rubber or hair, and a couple of blades of different sizes and shapes.

Spinning - A way of fishing using a closed-face or open-face spinning reel; reel is installed on the rod underside; rod guides are located on the rod underside.

Split Shotting - Typically referred to as stitch fishing since you move the bait in increments no bigger than a sewing stitch and performed just as gradually and being patient is the trick. Utilize a little # 5 split-shot and crimp it around 18 inches over a light wire 1/0 or lighter little hook. Spinning tackle is a necessity. Little worms are best for the mild application needed.

Spook - The act of startling a fish in an unfavorable manner. Instances: too much noise, casting a shadow.

Stick-Up - Fixed structure - limb, stump, pipe part, fence post - which extends around 5 feet or less over the surface; a preferred casting target of bass anglers.

Stragglers - Bass that stay near the coast after a general migration.

Stringer - Old-fashioned worm for a limitation of fish, utilized by competitive anglers to show their catch (10-pound stringer = 10 pounds of fish). Not in fact utilized any more to keep bass, simply a term individuals can't appear to stop utilizing.

Structure - Modifications in the shape of the lake bottom, impoundments or rivers, particularly those that affect fish habits. This is most likely the most misconstrued word when it comes to bass fishing. Structure is a feature on the lake bottom. Certain instances of structure are humps, creeks, sandbars, depressions, ledges, roadbeds and drop-offs. Some instances which are not structure: a tree, stump or brush pile.

Suspended Fish - Bass at mid depths, neither on the bottom nor close to the surface.

Swimming Lures - Sinking-type synthetic baits created to look like a swimming baitfish. Such plugs wobble and/or vibrate throughout retrieve; some have integrated rattles. Additionally referred to as lipless crankbaits.

Tail-Spinners - Lead-bodied, compact lures with a couple of spinner blades connected to a treble hook suspended from the body, and the tail; developed to look like an injured shad; helpful on schooling bass.

Taper - A location in water which slopes towards deeper depths.

Terminal Tackle - Angling tools, leaving out synthetic baits, connected to the fishing line end; instances consist of snaps, hooks, snap-swivels, swivels, drifts, sinkers and plastic beads.

Texas Rig - The technique of fastening a hook onto a plastic bait - lizard, worm, or crawfish, to ensure that the hook is without weeds. A slip sinker is threaded onto the line, and after that, a hook is connected to the line end. The hook is then placed into the worm head for approximately one-quarter of an inch and brought through up until just the eye is still embedded in the worm. The hook is, after that, spun and the point is ingrained somewhat into the worm without coming out the other side.

Thermocline - The water layer at which the temperature level shifts at least half a degree per foot of depth. Generally, a water layer where increasing cold and warm water meet.

Tight-Action Plug - A bait with brief, fast side-to-side motion.

Tiptop - Line guide at top of the fishing pole.

Topwaters - Drifting tough baits which produce certain degree of surface disruption throughout retrieve.

Trailer Hook - The additional hook, or cheater hook included in a single-hook lure, like a weedless spoon or a spinnerbait.

Transition - The imagined line where one bottom material type changes to another.

Treble Hook - Hook with bundled or single shaft and 3 points.

Triggering - Utilization of any lure-retrieval method or other fishing method that induces bass to attack.

Trolling Motor - A little electrical fishing motor, usually installed on the bow, which is utilized as secondary boat propulsion, for boat placement, and to navigate silently in fishing locations.

Turnover - The duration when the cold water on the water surface comes down and is substituted by warmer water from beneath.

Vertical Motion - Down and up motion of fish. It could additionally be a motion of a lure like a spoon.

Weedless - A lure created to be fished in thick cover with a slightest degree of snagging.

Weedline - Sudden weedbed edge brought on by an alteration in bottom type, depth or other aspects.

Wormin - The activity of fishing using a lizard, plastic worm, crawfish, or comparable bait.

I hope that you enjoyed reading through this book and that you have found it useful. If you want to share your thoughts on this book, you can do so by leaving a review on the Amazon page. Have a great rest of the day.

Printed in Great Britain
by Amazon